HANDMADE AT HOME
BUTTON AND BEAD
JEWELRY

**Please check all items for damages
before leaving the Library.
Thereafter you will be held
responsible for all injuries
to items beyond reasonable wear.**

HANDMADE AT HOME

BUTTON AND BEAD
JEWELRY

25 step-by-step projects

DEBORAH SCHNEEBELI-MORRELL

CICO BOOKS
LONDON NEW YORK

Published in 2011 by CICO Books
An imprint of Ryland Peters & Small
519 Broadway, 5th Floor,   20–21 Jockey's Fields,
New York NY 10012   London WC1R 4BW
www.cicobooks.com

10 9 8 7 6 5 4 3 2 1

The projects in this book were originally published by CICO Books
in *Bead & Button, Ribbon & Felt Jewelry* and *Big Bead Jewelry*.

Text and projects copyright © Deborah Schneebeli-Morrell 2006,
2007, 2011
Design, photography, and illustration copyright © CICO Books 2006,
2007, 2011

A CIP catalog record for this book is available from the Library
of Congress and the British Library.

ISBN 978-1-907563-74-4

Printed in China

Editor: Gillian Haslam
Designer: Fahema Khanam
Photographers: Heini Schneebeli and
Gloria Nicol (pages 16, 23, 64, and 66)
Stylist: Deborah Schneebeli-Morrell
Illustrator: Kate Simunek

Contents

Introduction

The concept of jewelry is changing as people move away from the traditional idea that only semi-precious stones can be classified as proper jewelry. Anything goes, and the trend is inventive and flamboyant. It is as if there has been an explosion of ideas, a borrowing of techniques, a reference to other cultures, and a re-invention of the very term "jewelry"!

Look around you, in clothes stores as well as in specialist outlets, in magazines and fashion photos, and study the jewelry worn by other people. You will see extraordinary combinations with all kinds of fabric and trimmings used as an integral part of the jewelry.

This inspiring book provides you with the techniques and ideas to create your own enduring quality pieces to rival any store-bought item. Whilst making the pieces, your own imagination will be provoked, you will have your own ideas and develop a sense of color, and I hope you will go on to experiment with exciting new designs of your own. Jewelry makes a wonderful gift, and by making your own you can tailor your piece to suit the recipient—everyone loves to receive a handmade present. There are no rules—a little patience, a modicum of skill, and a burning desire to make something yourself instead of buying it are all that is needed.

Equipment

Tools

What is unique about the projects in this book is how few specialist tools are needed. Two pairs of jewelry-making pliers are essential—chain-nosed pliers for pressing crimp beads flat and round-nosed pliers for turning wire into small loops—for example, to attach an end pin securely to a chain. No other specialist equipment is needed, but it will be useful to have an ordinary pair of scissors, a measuring tape, and a large sewing needle (also known as a chenille needle) for threading beading elastic.

Probably the most useful item to have in your kit is a beading mat made from a synthetic material with a soft pile. Place your beads here so they are easy to see and will not roll away.

Materials

The good thing about making jewelry from everyday materials is that fabrics, ribbons, buttons, and beads are so readily available. They may even have been collected over the years just because small scraps, often with great patterns, colors, textures, and, not least, memories, may be hard to throw away. If you don't have access to these inherited domestic objects, it is quite easy to find buttons and fabric in flea markets, thrift stores, and rummage or jumble sales.

Making jewelry in this way, with these modest materials, is somehow an extension of the principles of patchwork—to waste nothing and to transform, with patience and skill, an ordinary everyday material into something useful and beautiful.

Buttons

Some people are lucky enough to have inherited a sewing box or a box of buttons. These are often handed down from mother to daughter to granddaughter and are treasured items, although very rarely are they used. During the days when most clothes were sewn at home, the button box would have been full of an array of different kinds of buttons. Shirt buttons in particular were always made from mother of pearl, and the larger examples are now collectors' pieces, but even rather more ordinary everyday buttons can be put to creative use.

Beads

Flea markets, antique markets, and retro stores are all brilliant places to find inspiring strings of beads or necklaces at a low cost which you can dismantle and then use the elements to redesign into a unique piece of your own jewelry. Surprisingly, it can be less costly to do this than sourcing beads direct from a supplier. One important consideration when buying your beads is to make sure the central threading hole is large enough to take your chosen cord. Beads with really large holes are less common.

There are now so many bead stores and websites where you can browse for beads. The choice is quite unbelievable, with beads originating from all over the world. You can spend as little or as much as you can afford; either way, it is possible to create an original piece to a professional standard.

Do try to visit bead stores, too, as they are the most inspiring places. Good bead stores are staffed by knowledgeable enthusiasts and usually many examples of made-up jewelry are on show as an inspiration and a guide to new customers and novice beaders.

The sensitive use of color, size, texture, and form in the mix of beads and stones and good design are the key elements in making a striking piece of jewelry. The projects in this book will introduce you to these concepts and techniques and enable you to make your own jewelry.

Semi-precious stones

Nothing can match the beauty of semi-precious stones. Even before you touch, see, or feel them, the names are so evocative and poetic. Lapis lazuli, lemon jade, turquoise, amazonite, rose quartz, moonstone, agate, amethyst, and serpentine—these are only a few of the extensive list of possibilities conveniently available today.

Many bead suppliers and stores sell semi-precious stones that have been fashioned into beads of all shapes and sizes and they are usually fairly inexpensive, the larger examples

naturally being the most costly. However, they are well within the budget of most people and can be used to create an exquisite piece of jewelry a fraction of the price of a similar piece in a store.

Glass beads

The variety of glass beads can be quite dazzling at times. Some are chunky, recycled glass, which looks like it has been worn by the tides in the sea, whereas others are figured and highly decorated, in particular the millefiori beads which are made in Italy, the home of exquisite glass bead-making for centuries. Some lovely and inspiring examples have a silver foil lining encased within the bead, bringing a reflective, shimmering quality to the glass. These are often shaped and come in a huge variety of sizes.

Tiny glass seed beads are often referred to as rocailles. They come in many colors, both transparent and matte as well as metallic, and are particularly effective when used in conjunction with larger and more decorated feature beads. For a beginner, it may be worth buying a bead collection (these often feature the less expensive Indian beads, which can be highly decorative).

Pearls

Of all the beads available, none can really surpass the beauty and elegance of a single pearl, which has always been a classic style favorite. Cultured freshwater pearl strings, which are produced in the Far East, are available in a range of sizes, and as well as the natural color, a wide choice of subtly dyed tones can be found. Some may be quite irregular in shape and others elongated, but all these variations help to add interest and enhance the quality of pearly iridescence. Although a little more expensive than most beads, they are not beyond the pocket of most people, especially if you shop around. It is often possible to see them piled high in flea markets or antique markets at very reasonable prices.

Other beads with pearl-like qualities are the disks cut from mother-of-pearl or abalone shell. These are often drilled with a central or off-center hole and look exquisite knotted onto pale silk thread or almost invisible nylon monofilament. One or two of the projects in the book use a complete shell—these often have drilled or natural holes in which other pearls or complementary beads can be threaded. Although a little expensive to buy, they can be easily fashioned into a striking pendant.

Felt

Never throw away a worn-out sweater if you like the color—launder it on a very hot cycle in the washing machine to felt it. It makes an excellent material to work with and is particularly attractive when appliquéd and embroidered with a fine silk or chenille ribbon. Simpler patterned calicos can be cut into circles, sewn into little pouches that can be stuffed with batting, and made into beads, or constructed into a patchwork decorated with buttons.

Cords, ribbons, and wire

To make a varied collection of stylish jewelry, you will need to use a variety of cords, threads, wires, rat tail, leather, suede, beading elastic, tiger tail, nylon monofilament, and ribbons. Luckily, most beading suppliers will have a comprehensive selection of all these essential items.

Findings

Jewelry findings come in a variety of metals, including silver, gold, plated metal, copper, and bronze. You will need a variety of clasps, jump rings and split rings, calottes, crimp beads and tubes, end pins, and eye pins. Earring "fish" hooks have been used in this book, although you could easily substitute other forms of earring attachments for those without pierced ears. It is best to use sterling silver or copper chains, as a pure metal always looks better and is easier to work with.

However, you can also make clever use of textiles and trimmings. For example, a clasp for closing a necklace or bracelet can be replaced by a judicious and decorative tie of a ribbon or the knotting of a thread or cord. A button or bead and ribbon loop also makes an excellent fastening.

Patchwork Circle Necklace

Silk Ribbon Bracelet with Pearl Buttons

Most people possess a sewing box full of buttons, threads, and scraps of fabric. Some of us also create patchwork or do a form of embroidery, crochet, or knitting—and all these activities provide leftover materials and scraps that we store for future projects. This chapter shows how to transform these elements into fashionable and original jewelry that will rival any store-bought versions and will add color and flair to any outfit.

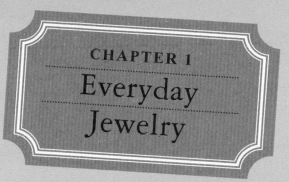

CHAPTER 1

Everyday Jewelry

Pink Pompom
Necklace

Patchwork Circle Necklace

MATERIALS

5 circles of pink fabric in different patterns, each 3½in (9cm) in diameter

Needle and strong thread

5 assorted buttons to complement the fabric, each approximately 1in (2.5cm) in diameter

10 smaller assorted buttons, approximately ¾in (1.5cm) in diameter

Jeweler's copper wire, 0.6mm or 0.8mm thickness

Double link copper chain, 18in (45cm) long

2 copper jump rings, ⅜in (8mm) in diameter

Copper lobster clasp

Wire cutters

Round-nosed pliers

Flat-nosed pliers

Scissors

In this project, a traditional decorative patchwork technique has been reworked to provide unusual elements in this fashionable necklace. Pretty printed fabric circles with complementary patterns are gathered into little "parcels," while the addition of decorative buttons to both sides hides the sewing stitches and gives a neat fixing for threading the copper wire which, in turn, attaches the circles to the fine copper chain. The combination of sewing and jewelry-making techniques can produce some really interesting pieces.

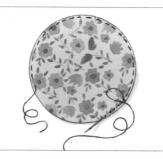

1 Sew a neat running stitch around the outer edge of the fabric circles using the needle and thread.

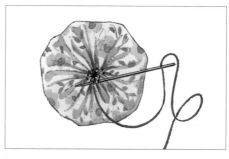

2 Pull the thread to gather the edge of the circle tightly together. Make a few holding stitches to secure the gathers and cut off the remaining thread.

Patchwork Circle Necklace 13

3 Place a large button over the gathered center of the circle and hold a smaller button on the back. Thread a 5in (12.5cm) length of copper wire through one of the holes in the front button, push it through the fabric, and out through one of the holes in the back button. Fold the wire against the fabric and thread each end through a hole in another small button.

4 Push the button down to touch the edge of the fabric circle. Twist the wire tightly together, then cut off one of the ends close to the twist using the wire cutters.

5 Secure a jump ring at each end of the copper chain, attaching a lobster clasp to one side before closing the jump ring using the two pairs of pliers.

6 Attach the circles to the central part of the chain 2in (5cm) apart by looping the long end of the wire through a chain link. Turn the wire back on itself and twist around to secure. Cut off the excess with wire cutters.

Variation
Patchwork Corsage

This original corsage has been made using the same technique, although here the buttons have been attached using copper wire threaded with tiny matching seed beads and then passed through the button holes, to resemble flower stamens. The wires are twisted together on the back and the three flowers attached to a brooch pin.

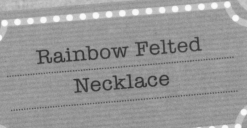

Rainbow Felted
Necklace

This richly colorful necklace is among the simplest projects in this book, and it is the skill in choosing the best combination of colors that makes it work so well. Wooden beads are easy to source, and you may even be able to re-use beads from a long-abandoned children's jewelry box. The felted wool squares are simply cut from old blankets or prettily colored sweaters which were destined for the thrift store. To make a pretty matching bracelet, use the same technique as for the necklace but thread only four squares of felted wool between small flower-painted wooden beads.

MATERIALS

Old woolen blankets or sweaters felted by washing
on a hot wash (in blue, pink, terra cotta, and orange)

Needle with a large eye (also known as a chenille needle)

Beading elastic ½in (0.8mm) thick, approximately
32in (80cm) long

16 bright pink wooden spacer beads

8 large oval wooden beads

Large silver-colored crimp bead

Scissors

Chain-nosed pliers

Crafter's tip Save all sorts of
fabric for this project, such as old
patchwork pieces, worn blankets, or
moth-eaten sweaters. You can always
salvage enough from the original item
for a really interesting project. Work with
the colors you find, or you may like to
dye fabric to match your beads. A really
hot wash will easily felt any kind of wool
(launder the woolen garment before
cutting it into squares).

1 Cut out freehand 24 squares,
approximately ¾in (2cm) square, in each
of the four colors of the felted wool.

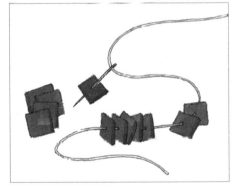

2 Thread the needle with the elastic and
start to push through the center of 12 pieces
of felt in your first color.

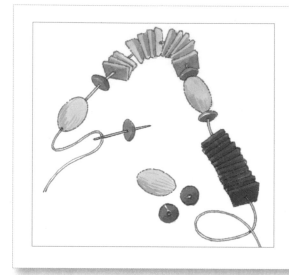

3 Follow with a pink spacer bead, a blue oval bead, and another pink spacer. Next, thread on 12 more pieces of felt in a different color. Repeat until you have used up all the beads and felt.

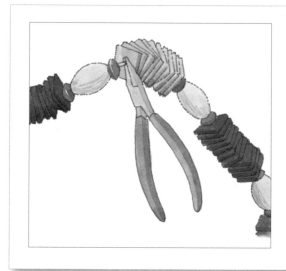

4 Thread the crimp bead onto one end of the elastic, pull to stretch it over your finger, and slide the other end through the bead. Pull firmly so that the necklace is tight with no elastic visible, then press the crimp closed with the pliers. Cut off the elastic ends and conceal the join inside one of the big beads.

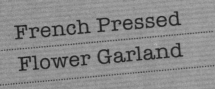

French Pressed
Flower Garland

This charming garland is perfect for a sunny summer's day. The felt flowers, simply threaded on a garland of spring-green seed beads, were traditionally used in hat decoration and are now being used with renewed interest by clothes designers and jewelers. They are supplied in small bundles from a good haberdashery or notions store or ribbon emporium.

MATERIALS

2 small silver crimp tubes, 1/16in (1.3mm)

1 yard (1m) tiger tail

Green seed beads, approximately 1/8in (3mm) in diameter

7 viola felt flowers, 1 1/4in (3cm) in diameter

7 mauve felt daisies, 1in (2.5cm) in diameter

Flat-nosed pliers

Scissors

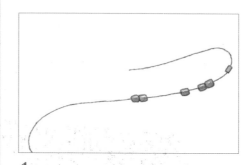

1 Attach a precautionary crimp tube at one end of the tiger tail. Thread approximately five green seed beads onto the tiger tail.

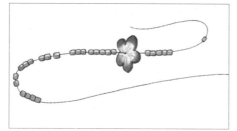

2 Next, thread on a felt flower, followed by approximately 20 more seed beads.

3 Add a different shaped flower and continue threading another 20 or so seed beads after it.

4 When 14 flowers have been threaded in place, add about 10 beads after the last flower. Cut off the precautionary crimp tube and discard. Bring the two ends of the tiger tail together through the new crimp tube and pull fairly tight (but allow the beads some room to move or the necklace will not hang properly). Press to secure with the flat-nosed pliers. Cut off the excess, leaving a small length to hide inside the adjoining seed beads.

Variation
French Pressed Flower Earrings

Use any leftover flowers to make a pretty pair of matching earrings using ready-made ear hooks. You could also follow the main project but use a smaller amount of tiger tail to make a bracelet and create a matching set.

Stretchy Button
Bracelet

MATERIALS

Assortment of 20 red-toned buttons in varying sizes

20 orange opaque glass beads

Clear beading elastic ½in (0.8mm) thick, approximately 20in (50cm) long

Scissors

Large crimp bead

Chain-nosed pliers

This is another very simple project which gives a stylish result. There can hardly be any crafters who do not own a button box—and, of course, lovely buttons are still readily available to buy so you can design any colorway you want. To make the bracelet shown here, choose an assortment of buttons in all tones of red, from pink through to burnt orange.

1 Thread the beads and buttons alternately onto the length of beading elastic until all have been used up.

2 Thread one end of the elastic through the crimp bead. Pull the elastic tight by wrapping it around your finger and thread the other end through. Pull both ends and press the crimp bead with pliers to secure. Cut off the ends neatly.

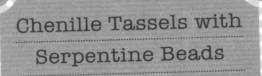

These gorgeous chenille tassels can be purchased from good sewing, haberdashery, or notions stores—they are often used to adorn cushions, pillows curtains, lampshades, and other home decorating projects. They are so tactile and work beautifully with other materials when incorporated into imaginative jewelry designs. The subtle shades of rust brown and pea green are complementary and blend stunningly with the natural tones of the jade and serpentine beads. The necklace is long enough to fit over the head and is threaded on beading elastic, avoiding the need for any fastening.

MATERIALS

1 yard (1m) clear beading elastic, ½in (0.5mm) thick

Chenille needle (with an eye large enough to take the elastic, but small enough to fit through the smallest bead when threaded)

2 gold-colored crimp tubes, ¹⁄₁₆in (2mm) in diameter

9 small green seed beads, ⅛in (3mm) in diameter

30 small lemon jade cubes

5 teardrop jade beads, ¼in (6mm) in diameter

24 elongated serpentine beads, ⅝in (1.5cm) in diameter

2 green chenille tassels

1 rust chenille tassel

Scissors

Flat-nosed pliers

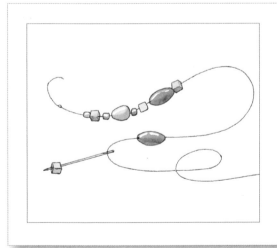

1 Thread the elastic through the needle. Fix a precautionary crimp bead to one end of the elastic to stop the threaded beads falling off. Thread on a seed bead, followed by a lemon jade cube, another seed bead, and then a teardrop jade bead and a seed bead. Thread on another jade cube, then an elongated serpentine bead. Continue threading the serpentine and jade cubes alternately until ten serpentine beads are in place, finishing with a cube.

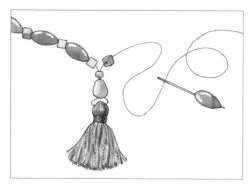

2 After the last cube, add a green seed bead, followed by a teardrop jade bead. Push the needle through the top of the green tassel and bring the elastic back on itself through the same teardrop bead, followed once more by the seed bead. Open out the elastic and add a jade cube. Continue with two serpentine beads, ending once more with a cube.

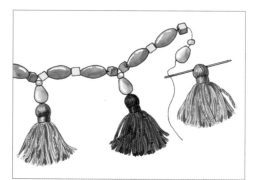

3 Continue by adding the rust tassel in the same way, followed by the second green one, until all three tassels are in place, with the central rust one flanked by the two green ones.

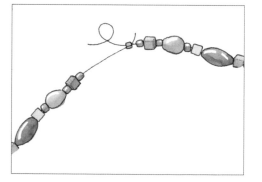

4 Thread the remaining beads in exactly the same way as at the beginning of the necklace. Cut off the temporary crimp tube and thread the two ends of the elastic through the new crimp tube and press to secure with flat-nosed pliers. Cut off the elastic ends, leaving ½in (1cm), and hide the ends in the adjacent beads.

Variation
Jasper and Amethyst Bracelet

Once you start to work with semi-precious stones, you will marvel at the stunning variety of color, texture, and form in the stones extracted from the earth and rock beneath us. These stones form some of the most ancient beads. This unusual little bracelet, using jasper and amethyst beads, is made in the same way as the main project. The beads are subtly complemented with a mauve tassel.

Antique Lace
Necklace

MATERIALS

Iron-on, double-sided dressmaking adhesive

Antique lace, 12 x 12in (30 x 30cm)

Iron

Thick interfacing, 12 x 6in (30 x 15cm)

Light-colored felt pen

Scissors

3 yards (3m) of black-and-white
chequered ribbon, ½in (1cm) wide

Hole punch

13 white plastic beads, ¾in (2cm) in diameter

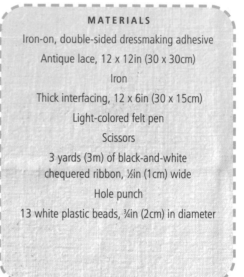

Using interfacing and iron-on adhesive in this necklace has eliminated the need for any stitching. The lace circles are easy to make—the lace is bonded to a stiffening fabric with a double-sided adhesive. The lace becomes stronger and will not unravel or fray. The combination of the lace and plain white beads threaded on black-and-white ribbon makes a bold, striking necklace.

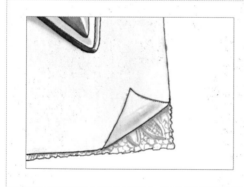

1 Following the manufacturer's instructions on the packaging, iron the double-sided adhesive (paper side up) to the wrong side of the lace square.

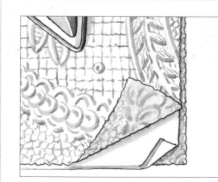

2 When the adhesive has cooled, cut the lace in half and remove the paper backing from the adhesive side of each piece of lace. Turn the lace adhesive side down, place on top of the interfacing, and iron. Turn the interfacing over and iron the other piece of lace to the reverse side, creating a sandwich of lace-interfacing-lace. Do make sure that the right side of the lace faces outward.

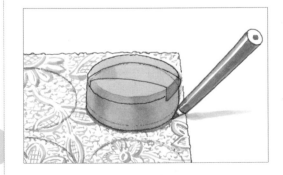

3 Using a circular item with a 1½in (4cm) diameter (such as the lid of a spice jar), draw around it on to the lace using a light-colored felt pen. Repeat to make 11 circles in total. Using sharp scissors, carefully cut out the circles just inside the pen outlines.

4 Use the hole punch to create a hole in each circle—you will need to press very firmly to make neat hole.

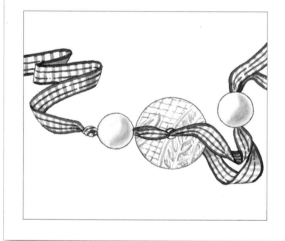

5 Cut the ribbon in half and lay the two lengths alongside each other. Tie a knot 8in (20cm) from one end of the double ribbon. Thread on a white bead, then open up the ribbon and thread one end over the front of the lace circle and through the central hole. Bring the other ribbon from underneath the disk and through the same hole, then pass the two ribbons over the other side of the lace circle and through the next bead.

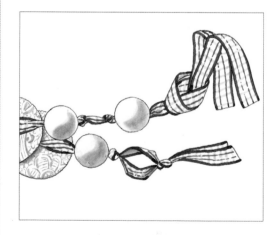

6 Continue threading the beads and disks in this manner until all the circles and 12 white beads are in place. After the last bead, tie a knot, leave a ¾in (2cm) gap and tie a further knot. Thread on a bead and tie a knot immediately after to hold in place. This makes the fastening bead. Repeat this sequence at the other end, but omit the last bead and instead leave a 1¼in (3cm) section of ribbon and tie a final knot. This makes the hole to enclose the bead at the other end.

Variation
Lace Disk Earrings on Wavy Braid

The lace disks are threaded in the same way as the necklace, but beads have been substituted for the buttons and the ribbon has been replaced by a wavy antique braid. This method of stringing lace disks, beads, buttons, and ribbon together would make a stylish, modern belt.

Crocheted Circles on Silk Ribbon

The crochet circles used here were discovered in my sewing box, left over from another project. They have been perfectly matched with crochet-covered beads, which can be found in a good bead store, and two strands of exquisite hand-dyed silk ribbon. This is a quick project to create, and if you enjoy making the necklace, why not learn to crochet and create your own designs and colorways?

MATERIALS

2 yards (2m) yellow/red hand-dyed silk ribbon, ½in (1cm) wide

2 yards (2m) pink hand-dyed silk ribbon, 1in (2.5cm) wide

5 small crochet circles, in orange and pale and deep pinks, approximately 1¼in (3cm) in diameter

Crochet hook

4 crochet-covered beads in pink and two-toned pink stripes, 1in (2.5cm) in diameter

4 large crochet circles, in the same colors, approximately 2in (5cm) in diameter

Scissors

1 Lay the two lengths of ribbon alongside each other and tie them together in a single knot 8in (20cm) from one end. Thread the narrower yellow/red ribbon over the front of the smaller orange crochet circle, then pull it through the central hole from behind with the help of the crochet hook. Bring the wider pink ribbon through the same hole from behind in the same manner.

2 Tie the two ribbons in a knot against the opposite side of the crochet circle, then make another knot after a further 2in (5cm). Thread on the first of the crochet beads, push it against the previous knot, and hold in place by tying a similar knot on the other side of the bead.

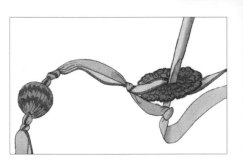

3 Leave another gap of 2in (5cm) after the bead and tie another knot, then thread the ribbons through the larger pink crochet circle in exactly the same manner as the first one. Always use the crochet hook to pull the ribbons through from each side.

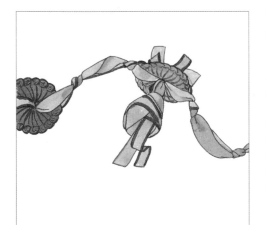

4 Tie a knot tightly against the pink circle and continue threading the ribbons, beads, and remaining crochet circles. Vary the order of color and the length of ribbon between the knots. When all four beads, three small crochet circles, and the remaining large ones are in place, tie a knot, leave a further 2in (5cm), and then tie another knot. Feed the two ribbon ends through the last small crochet circle; repeat at the other end threading the ribbons through from the other side. Knot the two ribbon lengths coming through from each side and cut off the ribbon ends, leaving ¾in (1.5cm) tails.

Chiffon Flower
Necklace

Pale blue chiffon flowers float delicately along fine silk ribbon. The chiffon flowers, purchased from a ribbon supplier, come in small packs which contain a large number of petals. They are used in dressmaking as decorative accessories, but adapt beautifully as elements in this magical garland. Three layers of chiffon petals are laid on top of each other to make the flowers. A bead on an endpin holds the petals in place in front, while a bead cap and a dab of glue hold them behind the flower. Small blue glass beads are attached through simple knots in the ribbon.

MATERIALS

6 assorted blue glass beads, approximately ½in (1cm) in diameter

10 small blue glass beads, ¼in (5mm) in diameter

11 gold-colored endpins

5 gold-colored bead caps

15 layers of pale blue chiffon flowers

5 tiny turquoise seed beads

1 yard (1m) pale blue silk ribbon, ⅜in (8mm) wide

1 yard (1m) toned olive green silk ribbon, ⅛in (3mm) wide

1 blue button with two holes, ¾in (1.5cm) in diameter

Round-nosed pliers

Flat-nosed pliers

Wire cutters

White craft glue

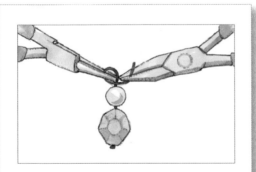

1 Thread an assortment of the blue glass beads onto endpins in pairs, with the larger shaped glass beads at the base. Using the round-nosed pliers, turn the excess endpin into a loop. Hold this loop with one pair of pliers and use the other pair to pull the end around on itself to make a secure twist. Cut off the excess with wire cutters. Make up six endpins in this way.

2 Thread an endpin through a turquoise seed bead, followed by a small glass bead. Follow this with the first layer of a chiffon flower, then add two more layers, adjusting the petals to make a flower. Turn the flower upside down and add a dab of glue followed by a bead cap, to secure the layers in place. Push down and turn the endpin into a loop as before. Cut off the excess wire. Make up five flowers in total.

3 Thread one flower centrally onto the two ribbons and tie the ribbons in a single knot around the loop.

4 Add a bead cluster on each side of this first flower, then tie the double ribbon in a single knot, enclosing the loop at the top of the bead cluster approximately 2¾in (7cm) away from the flower.

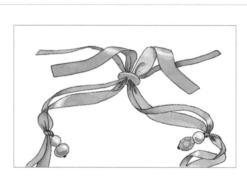

5 Add all the flowers and bead clusters in this manner, spacing them out evenly on each side of the central flower. Finish with a bead cluster (without a flower) at each end of the ribbons. Thread the double ribbons at each end through separate holes in the button, from the underside. At this stage you can adjust the length of the necklace.

6 Bring the double ribbon ends back through the opposite button holes (from the top) and tie into a double knot on the underside. Dab a spot of white glue on the knot for added security. Cut the ribbon about ¾in (2cm) from the ends, smear the cut edge with a little glue, and, when dry, cut again to give a neat finish.

Variation
Chiffon Flower Earrings

These feminine flower drop earrings are easy to make and match the garland beautifully. The bead at the base is threaded on to an endpin, and in order to make it swing freely, it is looped around the ring at the base of an eyepin, which has been threaded with a small blue glass bead. As in the necklace, the petals are lightly glued in place and a gold-colored bead cap follows on. Six assorted beads are threaded above the flower onto the length of the eyepin, which is itself looped around the base ring on a gold earring hook.

Silk Ribbon Bracelet
with Pearl Buttons

This brightly colored bracelet features shaped mother-of-pearl buttons threaded together with six strands of narrow silk ribbon. The vibrant shades of the ribbon give the bracelet a fun, summery appearance, but the design would work equally well using muted shades of gray and silver ribbon for a more sophisticated effect. No clasp has been used; instead, a button is cleverly used to slide along the ribbons, allowing you to adjust the size of the bracelet. A cross-grained rayon ribbon has been threaded through similar buttons for the bracelet shown on the right of the photograph. In both designs, the bracelets have been finished by knotting the ribbon ends after threading through additional buttons.

Crafter's tip Always check that the ribbon will fit through all the holes in your selected buttons.

1 Thread the needle with all six ribbons. Take the needle through the first hole of the button from the underside. Bring the needle back through the second hole, then slide the button along the ribbons until it sits in the center of them.

2 Continue threading the buttons in this manner, positioning two on each side of the central button and alternating the button shapes, until you have five buttons in place.

3 Bring the ribbons through the underside of the sixth button, threading six ribbons through each hole. This creates the slide fastener.

4 Cut the ribbon ends to leave tails of 3in (7.5cm), then thread another button onto the ends. Tie each bundle of ribbons into a neat single knot to hold this button in place and cut off the ends to leave ¾in (2cm) remaining.

Variation
Blue Chiffon Ribbon Bracelet with Pearl Buttons and Drop Beads

This charming bracelet is so simple to make. A single length of narrow chiffon ribbon has been carefully threaded through the smoky-toned mother-of-pearl buttons. The button slide fastener means there is no need to use a more conventional metal clasp. The design is enhanced by the use of pretty drop beads spaced between the buttons. This simple technique can easily be adapted to make a larger piece of jewelry, such as a matching necklace—just remember to select buttons with holes of a suitable size to accommodate the width of ribbon.

Pink Pompom Necklace

This stunning necklace with its random assortment of cotton pompoms, beads, buttons, and flowers on silk and satin ribbon and silk thread is a real statement in pink! Although it looks complicated, there are really no rules and each person will string this necklace differently. It is a wonderful project for using up an assortment of materials leftover after making other pieces of jewelry. The only thing to remember is to bring the ribbons together periodically in twos or threes into a knot between the threading of all the decorative elements.

MATERIALS

1½ yards (1.5m) pink silk pearl stringing thread, with threader attached

1½ yards (1.5m) brick red silk ribbon, ³⁄₁₆in (4mm) wide

1½ yards (1.5m) fuschia satin ribbon, ½in (1cm) wide

Needle with eye large enough to take the narrow silk ribbon

Selection of assorted beads, such as wooden beads, glass seed beads, shaped beads, etc

14 pink, red, and orange buttons in a variety of sizes

5 assorted silk flowers

Pink cotton pompoms, cut from braid

Scissors

White craft glue

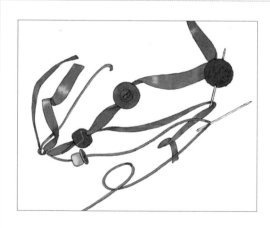

1 Lay all three lengths of ribbon/thread together and tie all three into a knot 4¾in (12cm) from one end (the threader on the pearl stringing thread should be at the other end). Thread the narrow silk ribbon into the needle. Thread a pink wooden bead onto the pink thread, followed by a small orange button, and tie a double knot after the button. Thread the satin and silk ribbons together through the square wooden bead, separate them, and thread the satin ribbon through a pink button so that it lies flat.

Pink Pompom Necklace 43

2 Knot the satin ribbon 2in (5cm) after the pink button, pass through the center of a silk flower, and immediately tie another knot to hold the flower on place. After ¾in (2cm), tie another knot and thread a pink wooden bead before tying a further knot. Thread the silk ribbon through the pink pompom and tie a double knot 1½in (4cm) from the orange button on the pearl thread. Follow with a group of beads and a further double knot. After ½in (1cm), tie the silk ribbon and silk thread together.

3 Continue threading the necklace in a random fashion with the flowers, larger beads, and buttons on the satin ribbon, the cotton pompoms and smaller buttons on the silk ribbon, and the smallest beads and buttons on the silk thread. Periodically bring these threads together in a knot to give cohesion to the necklace.

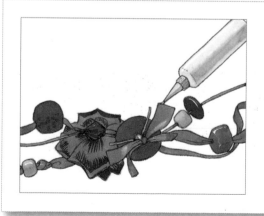

4 When the necklace is 1 yard (1m) long, finish off by tying the three cords into a knot at each end, and pass the two sets of ends through the two holes on a larger pink button from underneath. Tie them together on the right side of the button, add a dab of glue, and tie a second knot. Trim the ends and smear some glue along the cut. When dry, cut neatly again to prevent fraying.

Variation
Pink Pompoms, Buttons, and Beads

This simpler necklace with its ribbon-tie ends uses similar elements in a more economical way. The pretty selection of beads, buttons, and three sorts of cotton pompoms has been randomly threaded onto pale pink satin rat tail and a yellow pearl threading silk. This kind of necklace is an ideal project for using up spare beads and leftover threads.

Vintage Shirt
Button Necklace

These unremarkable, utilitarian white shirt buttons have been recovered from an inherited button box. There was a time when buttons would always have been retrieved when clothes were worn out, to be used on another garment. These vintage buttons have waited a long time but when rediscovered, their simple qualities helped design this rather clever, modern-looking necklace. It is incredibly straightforward to make—the pink and white ribbons are simply woven through the holes in the buttons and beads. As there are four holes in each button and the ribbons pass through the same hole, this has the effect of making the buttons sit deliberately off-center.

MATERIALS

2 yards (2m) silk ribbon in pink and white, ⅜in (8mm) wide

2 needles

26 matt white round glass beads, ⅜in (8mm) in diameter

25 white shirt buttons with four holes, ¾in (1.5cm) in diameter

Scissors

White craft glue

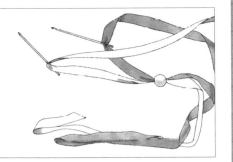

1 Thread each ribbon separately through a needle. Thread a white glass bead onto the ribbons approximately 12in (30cm) from the ends, by passing each needle separately through the hole in the bead. You will need to pull the ribbon tightly against the side of the bead hole in order to thread the second ribbon through.

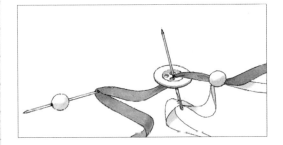

2 Add a button next to the bead on the long side of the ribbons. Do this by passing the pink ribbon over and through a hole in the button while passing the white ribbon through the same hole from underneath the button. Now bring the two ribbons together, white on top and pink beneath, and pass the two ends through another glass bead.

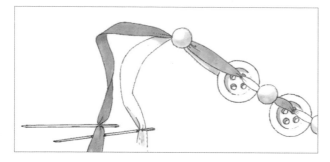

3 Continue threading in this manner until all 25 buttons and 26 glass beads are in place. You should finish with a glass bead at each end of the ribbons.

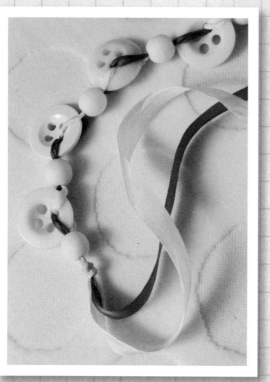

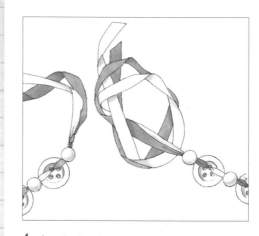

4 After the last bead, tie the two ribbons into a knot, leaving tails long enough (about 10in/25cm) to tie into a fastening bow. Add a smear of white glue to the ribbon ends to seal the threads; when dry, cut the ends neatly on a slant.

Variation
Long Swing Necklace with Buttons and Black Beads

This stylish, long swing necklace is particularly fashionable. The same white shirt buttons have been used but have been rather more sparsely threaded on black cord and white satin rat tail, alternating them with black plastic beads. The necklace has been cleverly finished by threading the cords through one of the buttons and knotting them on the other side. As always, add a dab of white craft glue to the cut ends of the cord to stop them fraying.

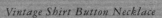

MATERIALS

Paper and pencil

Pins

Small scraps of indigo-dyed lightweight linen

8in (20cm) length of brown cross-grain ribbon

Needle with large eye

16in (40cm) length of brown silk ribbon,
$\frac{3}{16}$in (4mm) wide

1 decorated brown vintage button

Small quantity of cotton or polyester
batting (wadding)

1 brooch pin

Scissors

These charming little patchwork hearts are made from the smallest scraps of linen and are reminiscent of a lavender bag you would secrete in your linen drawer. The indigo blue heart with its rust-colored silk ribbon stitching has a small brooch pin sewn onto the back. The simplest decoration has been added in the form of a cross-grain ribbon bow with a vintage button accent. All the sewing has been done using a narrow silk ribbon as the thread. A small amount of cotton or polyester batting (wadding) has been added to give it a gently padded effect.

1 Fold the piece of paper in half and draw half a heart, butting up to the fold line of the paper. Cut out the heart and open up (it will form a complete, symmetrical heart). Pin the paper heart to a double thickness of linen. Cut neatly around the paper heart.

2 Working on one thickness of the fabric, take the cross-grain ribbon and arrange into three loops and two tails. Thread the needle with the narrow silk ribbon, bring the ribbon from behind, through the cross-grain bow, and through the underside of the button. Then bring the ribbon through another hole on the front of the ribbon, back through the ribbon bow, and through to the back. Come through once more so that the button is held by a crossed silk ribbon through the four holes in the button. Tie the ribbon in a double knot on the reverse to secure.

3 Sew the two sides of the heart together using the narrow silk ribbon in a running stitch ¼in (5mm) in from the edge of the heart. Leave a ¾in (2cm) gap on one side before finishing.

4 Push the batting (wadding) into this gap (a pencil is useful for pushing the batting into the corners) until the heart is loosely packed. Sew up the gap, finish off neatly on the wrong side and hide the end in the "hem." Finally, sew the brooch pin to the back using the same silk ribbon.

This colorful necklace is simple to make and ideal for all those buttons and beads leftover from other projects. Flexible waxed cord has been threaded with an assortment of green, pink, and red seed beads, punctuated with shaped beads and small buttons. Larger buttons have been strung on a green silk ribbon which weaves in and out and alongside the seed beads. As with many projects in this book, there is no need for complicated fastenings. When a necklace is long enough to fit over the head, hidden or decorative knots are easy and appropriate.

MATERIALS

1 yard (1m) waxed linen thread

Beading needle

Eclectic mix of red, green, and pink seed beads

Selection of approximately 20 shaped or feature beads

1 yard (1m) green silk ribbon, ⅜in (8mm) wide

Needle for the silk ribbon

Selection of approximately 23 colored buttons in a variety of sizes

Scissors

White craft glue

1 Thread the waxed linen thread through the needle and begin to thread on a random assortment of seed beads interspersed with the odd feature bead.

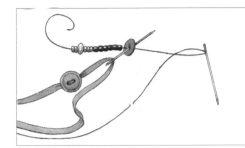

2 Thread the green silk ribbon through the other needle and thread one of the larger buttons into the center. Add a smaller button onto the beaded thread and pass the ribbon through the same button. On the opposite end, thread the ribbon through the larger feature bead, leaving the button to hang loosely on the ribbon.

3 Continue threading the necklace in this random manner, with beads on the thread and larger buttons along the ribbon.

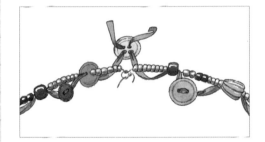

4 When the necklace has grown to a suitable length, thread the two ends of the silk through a four-hole button from the wrong side. Bring the ribbons back through the other holes and tie in a double knot, secured with a dab of white glue after the first knot. Cut off the excess ribbon, sealing the ends with a smear of white glue. At the same time, tie the thread with a double knot and hide the ends under adjoining beads.

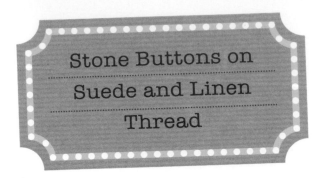

Stone Buttons on Suede and Linen Thread

MATERIALS

1½ yards (1.5m) natural suede thong, ¼in (5mm) in diameter

1½ yards (1.5m) linen thread

16 opaque glass beads, ½in (1cm) in diameter

9 stone disk buttons, ideally with fossils, 1¼in (3cm) in diameter

Scissors

White craft glue

Look closely at the stone disk buttons used for this necklace—they contain masses of tiny fossils. You may need to search around to find such lovely buttons, but you'll be amazed at the variety available. At one time all buttons were solely made from natural materials, such as stone, wood, horn, or bone. They are still made from these sources today and are relatively inexpensive to buy. A natural material such as stone needs to be threaded with an equally natural material, and here the linen thread and suede thong complement the subtle colors in the stone.

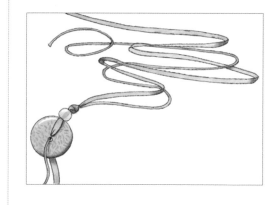

1 Lay the suede and linen parallel and tie them together in a knot 14in (35cm) from one end. Cut the suede thong at an angle for easy threading and add a touch of glue to the linen thread to stop it unravelling. Thread a glass bead on the two strands from the long ends, separate the threads, and take the suede thong over the front of the button and through the first hole. Bring the linen thread under the button and back through the second hole of the button.

2 Add another bead onto the double strands of suede and linen, then open out and thread another button in place. Continue threading in this manner (with a bead between each button) until nine buttons are in place. Add one more bead and tie a knot closely against it to hold all the buttons in place.

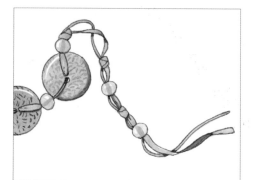

3 Working at one end, tie another knot 1¼in (3cm) from the last bead, thread another bead and after another 1¼in (3cm), tie another knot. After this knot add one last bead. Repeat this pattern on the other end of the necklace.

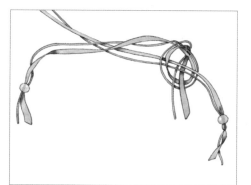

4 To make a sliding knot, lay the two sets of threads/thongs alongside each other. Turn one pair into a circle around the other pair, bring them around the back and through the circle, and pull to tighten to make the knot. Repeat on the other side. The gap between the sliding knots should be approximately 4in (10cm). Cut the ends to 2¾in (7cm), thread on a last glass bead and tie a holding knot in the end. Cut off the excess to leave tails of ½in (1cm).

Variation

Stone Buttons on a Green Suede Thong

The beautiful polished bone buttons used here have been threaded and knotted onto a spring-green suede thong. When you have strong elements such as texture, form, and color, sometimes it is a good idea to use them in a simple, restrained way for the best effect.

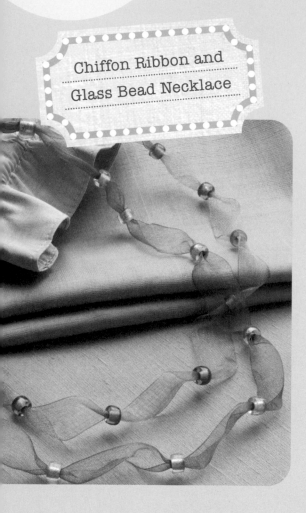

Chiffon Ribbon and
Glass Bead Necklace

Ribbon Rosebud
Corsage

While still using the same basic elements of beads, buttons, fabric, and ribbon, the projects in this chapter show how you can create stunning handmade jewelry with the "wow" factor. Semi-precious stones and glass and pearl beads can be expensive to buy, but when used in small quantity and combined with other elements, they become quite affordable. As always, it is your choice of materials and their combination that makes a good piece of jewelry.

CHAPTER 2
Evening Jewelry

Abalone Button Bracelet

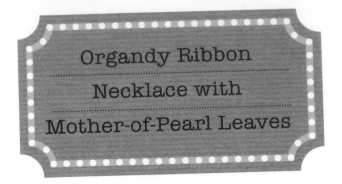

Organdy Ribbon Necklace with Mother-of-Pearl Leaves

MATERIALS

1 yard (1m) lengths of organdy ribbon in cream, mauve, and pink, ³⁄₁₆in (4mm) wide

Needle (check it fits through the holes in the leaves)

36 mother-of-pearl leaves, drilled with holes

2 small pink glass beads

2 silver calottes

2 silver jump rings, ³⁄₁₆in (4mm) and ¼in (6mm) in diameter

1 silver snake clasp

Scissors

Flat-nosed pliers

Round-nosed pliers

White craft glue (optional)

These shimmering mother-of-pearl leaves have been cut from an abalone shell and can be bought in long strands. These particular leaves have a single hole drilled at the top, allowing the narrowest of organdy ribbons to be threaded through. Each leaf is fixed in place along the length of the ribbon by single knots and all three strands of ribbon are brought together through a single pink glass bead at each end. Using three strands of ribbon in complementary colors means a generous number of leaves can be threaded, creating a sumptuous effect.

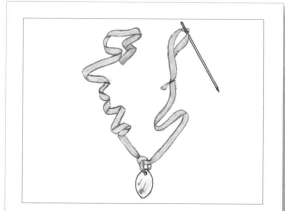

1 Thread the needle with the first length of ribbon, thread through the hole at the top of a leaf shape, and tie the ribbon around in a single knot to hold in place roughly in the center of the ribbon.

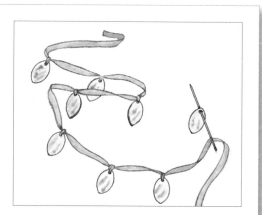

2 Tie on more leaves in the same way on either side of this central leaf, spacing them about 1½in (4cm) apart, until you have knotted 12 leaves in place.

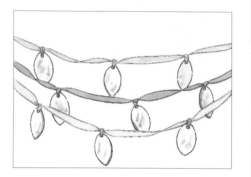

3 Repeat this same process on the other two lengths of ribbon, adjusting the width of the knots so that the leaves will appear evenly along the three ribbons when placed alongside each other.

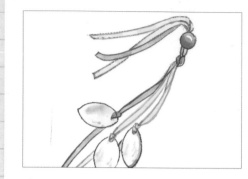

4 Bring the three lengths of ribbon together at the ends and tie into a knot, then thread the ends through one of the pink glass beads.

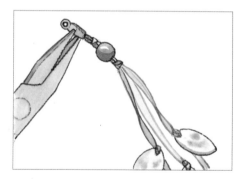

5 Tie another knot just after the pink bead and cut off the ribbons so that the ends just fit into the calotte. You can add a dab of glue here for extra security, if you wish. Close the calotte over the ribbon ends with the flat-nosed pliers.

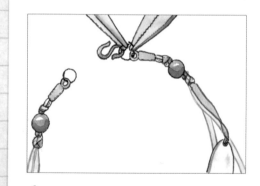

6 Repeat with another pink bead and calotte on the other end of the necklace. Add the two jump rings to each of the rings on the calottes. Add the snake clasp to the smaller jump ring and close firmly using both pairs of pliers.

Organdy Ribbon Necklace with Mother-of-Pearl Leaves

Large mother-of-pearl buttons have been used here to create these beautiful, shimmering earrings. The large buttons were discovered in an inherited button box and the slightly smaller ones were bought from a haberdashery or notions store. The method of stringing them together is simple if a little fiddly, but you soon find that working with such lovely materials is a pleasure in itself. The trick is to thread them so the buttons lie flat and in line with each other.

MATERIALS

Nylon monofilament thread, approximately
0.3mm thick

8 clear round beads, ⅛in (3mm) in diameter

10 small mother-of-pearl shirt buttons

2 large mother-of-pearl buttons, approximately
1¼in (3cm) in diameter

2 smaller mother-of-pearl buttons, approximately
¾in (2cm) in diameter

A small handful of the smallest clear seed beads
you can find

2 silver earring fish hooks

2 silver crimp tubes, ⅛in (3mm) in diameter

Chain-nosed pliers

Scissors

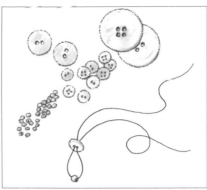

1 Cut a 12in (30cm) length of the nylon monofilament and thread a single clear round bead centrally on it. Fold the nylon in half and thread each end through separate holes in a small shirt button.

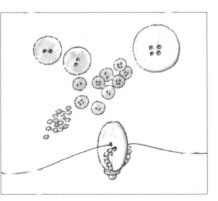

2 Open out the two strands and thread each one with enough seed beads to reach the same hole on each side of the large button. Push the nylon thread through from each side and pull to tighten all the beads.

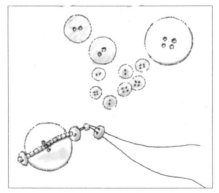

3 Thread each side again with enough seed beads to reach the top of the button, bring them together and thread through separate holes in the next shirt button. Follow this with a small round bead, followed by another shirt button.

Pearl Button Earrings 65

4 Repeat the same threading method, this time using the smaller pearl button. When you have reached the top, thread on a shirt button, then a round bead, then another shirt button. Next, add a crimp tube, followed by a final round bead. Thread the nylon through the loop at the base of the earring hook, then back through the last bead and crimp tube. Pull tightly and press the crimp tube firmly with the pliers to secure. Cut off the excess nylon. Repeat the steps for the second earring.

Variation
Pearl Button Necklace

This necklace is made in a similar way but using a different color scheme. The matte browns of the rather ordinary buttons are cleverly set off against the threading of glittering mauve delica beads, spaced with small round amethyst beads.

Charm Bracelet with Woven Silk Ribbons

A charm bracelet is one of jewelry's great classics—it never goes out of fashion. This is partly because the charms are often mementoes or presents and thus have a personal significance, with many people collecting and adding to their charm bracelets over time. The silver and copper charms used here are readily found in specialist bead stores and are inexpensive to buy. The addition of the double silk ribbon, weaving itself through the links of the small copper chain, makes a conventional piece of jewelry really decorative and unusual.

MATERIALS

8in (20cm) length of small-link copper chain
(or a size to fit comfortably around your wrist)

1 copper jump ring, ⅛in (3mm) in diameter

1 small copper lobster clasp

14 copper jump rings, ¼in (5mm) in diameter

13 assorted charms, including 6 copper discs

2 small copper box calottes

2 oval jump rings, ⅛in (3mm) in diameter

16in (40cm) each pink and red narrow silk ribbon,
⅛in (3mm) wide

9 pink seed beads

2 needles with large eyes

Flat-nosed pliers

Round-nosed pliers

Wirecutters

White craft glue

1 Open out a small jump ring and link around the last link at one end of the chain, passing it through the small ring on the lobster clasp. Close tightly. It helps to hold the ring in place with one set of pliers whilst closing the ring with the others. Attach a large jump ring to the other end of the chain in the same manner.

2 Open out the remaining larger jump rings. Beginning at one end, attach the charms along the length of the chain, making sure you close the jump rings firmly around the chosen links to keep the charms secure.

3 Space the charms along the chain, interspersing the more solid charms with the copper discs. It is not necessary to count the links as it is better to measure the distance apart by eye, spacing them roughly ¾in (2cm) apart.

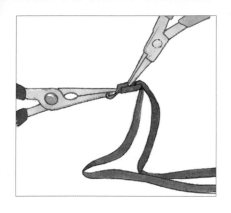

4 Lay the two ribbons on top of each other into the box calotte. Hold them in place with the round-nosed pliers whilst folding over the sides with flat-nosed pliers. Remove the round-nosed pliers and press very firmly to hold the ribbon securely. If you wish, add a tiny touch of glue before closing the calotte for extra security.

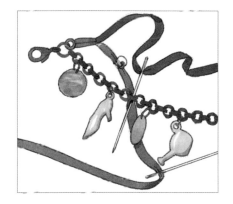

5 Attach the ring on the calotte to an oval jump ring and, in turn, attach this to the jump ring at the end of the chain. Thread the silk ribbons through the two separate needles. Thread a seed bead onto the red ribbon and tie in place with a single knot. Thread both ribbons through the same link of the chain after the second charm. Now thread and tie another seed bead onto the pink ribbon.

6 Weave the ribbons loosely in and out of the chain between the charms, adding a seed bead alternately to the red or pink ribbon. When you reach the other end, finish by securing the two ribbons into a box calotte, pressing tightly as before to secure. Attach to the jump ring at the other end of the chain.

Charm Bracelet with Woven Silk Ribbons

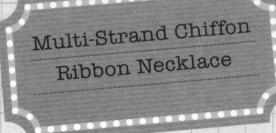

Multi-Strand Chiffon Ribbon Necklace

MATERIALS

Beading needle, with eye large enough to take ribbon

1½ yards (1.5m) lengths of chiffon ribbon in 8 different colors, ¼in (5mm) wide, plus an extra 4in (10cm) length in any one color

Selection of seed beads in yellow, pink, blue, orange, red, etc, 1⁄16in (2mm) in diameter

2 yellow foil-lined beads, 3⁄8in (8mm) in diameter

2 extra-large gold-colored crimp tubes (large enough to accommodate 16 ribbons)

1 snake clasp

2 gold-colored split rings, 3⁄8in (8mm) in diameter

7 green-gold pearl buttons, 5⁄8in (12mm) in diameter

Scissors

Flat-nosed pliers

Beading glue

This exquisite shimmering piece of jewelry is deceptively simple to make, if a little time-consuming. Eight strands of translucent shot chiffon ribbon in different colors have been threaded with tiny iridescent seed beads. The green-gold button accents are simply tied around the beaded ribbons, gathering them together to make delicate swags. The lightness of the tiny beads makes them appear to float on the narrow chiffon and consequently the necklace sits beautifully around the neck.

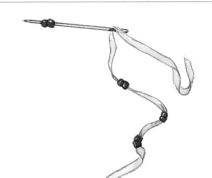

1 Thread the needle with the first length of chiffon ribbon. Thread on 80 identical seed beads, arranging them in pairs approximately ¾in (2cm) apart.

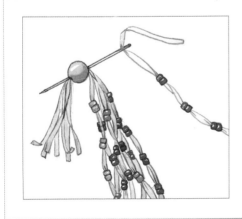

2 Thread the other seven strands of ribbon in the same way, changing the color of seed beads on each different color of ribbon. Bring all the threaded strands together at one end and pass them through the larger yellow bead. You will need to take each ribbon through individually with a needle.

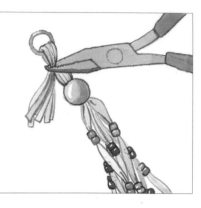

3 Take the eight ribbons through the large crimp tube and around the split ring. Bring the ribbons back through the crimp tube once more. You may have to push them through individually with the eye end of the needle. Pull through enough to push and hide the ends in the yellow bead. Press the crimp to secure the ribbons using the flat-nosed pliers. Add a dab of beading glue inside the yellow bead and push in the ribbon ends to secure.

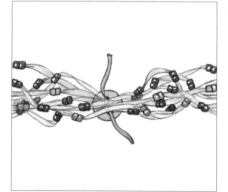

4 The necklace should measure about 20in (50cm) between the yellow beads. Add the snake clasp to the split ring at one end. Thread the short length of ribbon through the two holes on the right side of a button. Approximately 2in (5cm) from one end, gather the eight strands together, and tie the ribbon and button around tightly. Add a dab of glue on the knot and trim ends so they are hidden. Add all the other buttons along the necklace, roughly 2in (5cm) apart, facing the same way.

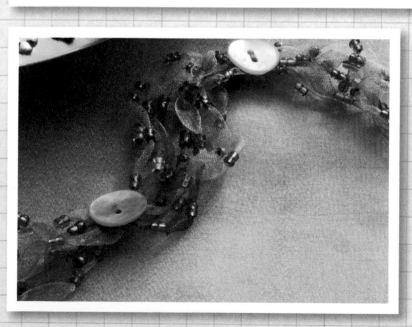

Abalone Button Bracelet

The pearly iridescence of the polished abalone shell has a magical property. It is one of the most extraordinary materials from the natural world, and as such has been prized for its rich decorative quality. It has many applications, including inlay in furniture (which was popular in the nineteenth century) and particularly its use in jewelry design. These buttons with the wonderfully deep tones come from New Zealand, where for generations this exquisite shell has been used in the art and craft of the Maori people.

MATERIALS

1 yard (1m) dip-dyed chiffon ribbon, 1¼in (3cm) wide

6 abalone buttons, 1¼in (3cm) in diameter

Tapestry needle

White craft glue

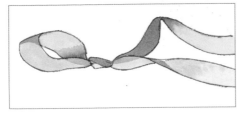

1 Fold the ribbon in half and tie a knot at the fold end to create a 1¼in (3cm) loop.

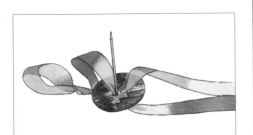

2 Push the first button up against the knot between the two strands of ribbon. Bring one end behind the button and through the second hole; take the other strand of ribbon over the front of the button and through the first hole.

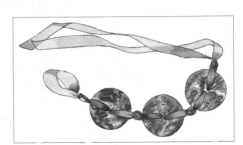

3 After the first button, tie the two ends of the ribbon into a single knot. Add another button, threading the two ends as before and tying a knot immediately after.

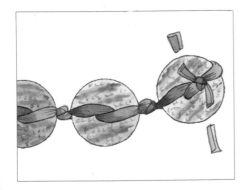

4 Continue threading in this manner until five buttons are in place, then tie another knot and add the last button. Instead of tying a knot after it, bring one end of the ribbon around the edge of the button toward the hole where the other ribbon emerges. Tie the ribbon tightly at this point into a double knot, adding a touch of glue after the first knot to secure. Cut off the excess ribbon ends so they are hidden by the button.

Shell Pendant on Satin Ribbon

This stunning project is so simple to make. There is little technique involved as the effect of the piece relies on using materials of the best quality. All it takes is a bold and beautiful large polished shell, some freshwater pearls, a sumptuous satin ribbon, and solid silver jump rings and clasp. The shell has the advantage of being able to be worn either way around—the concave side cradling the mother-of-pearl flower and the string of white freshwater pearls, or the reverse side displaying the simple natural beauty of the shell.

1 Thread the smallest jump ring through the hole in the shell flower and thread the three pearls onto the silver endpin. Turn the end over into a loop using the round-nosed pliers.

2 Fold the satin ribbon in half and push the fold through the hole in the shell from the concave side. Thread the large closed ring over the long ends and then feed these long ends through the ribbon loop on the back of the shell. Pull the loop up and over the top of the shell, arranging the folds as you go, and pull the ends tightly to hold the shell in place.

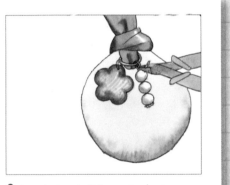

3 Attach the shell flower to the large silver ring around the ribbon by closing the jump ring. Feed the loop of the endpin holding the pearls over the same silver ring, bring it back on itself, and twist around the stem a couple of times using the flat-nosed pliers. Cut off the excess wire using the wire cutters.

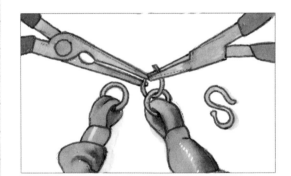

4 Thread the end of the ribbon through the ½in (1cm) closed ring and tie the ribbon into a knot approximately 8in (20cm) from the loop around the shell. Cut off the end of the ribbon at ¾in (2cm) and tuck out of sight behind the knot and in the gathering of the ribbon, smearing a small dab of glue along the cut edge of ribbon to prevent fraying. Repeat on the other side, this time attaching the ⅜in (7mm) jump ring to the large silver ring enclosed in the ribbon. Attach the snake clasp to the single ring to close.

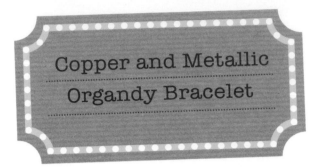

Copper and Metallic Organdy Bracelet

MATERIALS

8½in (22cm) length of copper chain

Copper jump ring, ¼in (5mm) in diameter

8 copper endpins, 2in (5cm) in length

10 assorted pink/red shaped glass beads

Offcut of copper metallic organdy

16in (40cm) clear beading elastic, ½in (0.8mm) thick

1 gold-colored crimp tube, ⅛in (3mm) in diameter

Sharp scissors

Flat-nosed pliers

Round-nosed pliers

Wire cutters

This pretty copper chain bracelet has no clasp—the technique is simply to make the chain circle large enough to slip over the wrist. A length of clear beading elastic has been threaded through the links and joined, pulling the chain in slightly so it won't slip off while being worn. This is a simple idea which avoids the need to attach a clasp. The shaped glass beads are easily attached using endpins and the finished bracelet is given a shimmering, lustrous quality by attaching short ties of copper-colored metallic organdy.

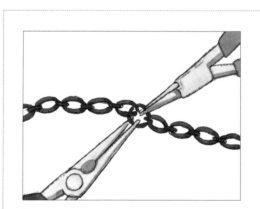

1 Join the length of chain together with the jump ring—you will need to use the two pairs of pliers, one to hold the ring while you close it with the other pair.

2 Thread the endpins through the glass beads (you can thread the smaller beads in pairs) and, using the round-nosed pliers, bend over the protruding wire to make the beginning of a loop. Attach the beads to the chain by threading this loop through the links, then turn the wire around on itself a couple of times and cut off the excess with the wire cutters. Attach the beads equidistantly around the chain.

3 Cut 20 lengths of the organdy, each measuring approximately 4in (10cm) long and ¾in (2cm) wide. Tie them in single knots evenly around the chain, through the individual links.

4 Thread the elastic through each link of the chain. Pull slightly to fit the wrist size and thread each end of the elastic through the opposite side of the crimp tube. Close the tube by pressing tightly with the flat-nosed pliers and cut off the excess ends.

Copper and Metallic Organdy Bracelet

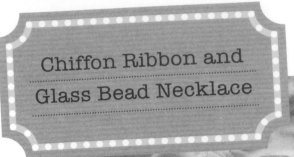

Chiffon Ribbon and Glass Bead Necklace

The shot green and bronze chiffon ribbons complement the foil-lined glass beads so well in this effective but simple project. The central hole in the bead needs to be just large enough to pass the threaded needle through, but narrow enough to hold the ribbon securely in place. Too large a hole means the beads slide out of place; too narrow and the needle will not pass through.

MATERIALS

Needle

28in (70cm) lengths of chiffon ribbon in blue-bronze and green-bronze, ½in (1cm) wide

11 pale green foil-lined glass beads with a ⅛in (3mm) diameter hole

10 smaller green foil-lined glass beads with a ⅛in (3mm) diameter hole

2 turquoise foil-lined glass beads with a ¼in (5mm) diameter hole

Gold-colored toggle clasp, ⅛in (8mm)

Beading glue

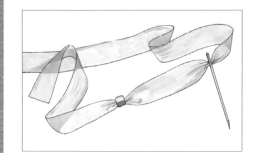

1 Thread the needle with the blue-bronze ribbon and thread the first pale green bead along the ribbon 4in (10cm) from one end.

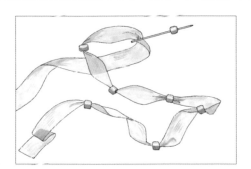

2 Continue threading the beads, leaving a gap of approximately 1½in (4cm) between beads until 11 beads are in place. Lay to one side.

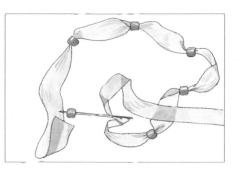

3 Take the green-bronze length of ribbon and thread in a similar manner with ten green beads.

4 Bring the two bead-threaded ribbons together and pass them both through a larger turquoise bead. Then pass these two ribbon ends through the ring on one side of the clasp.

5 Bring the double ribbon back on itself and tie into a knot. Repeat with the other two remaining ends, this time adding the toggle.

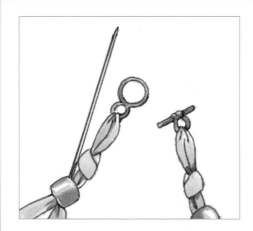

6 Using a needle, carefully dab some beading glue into the large bead and push the ribbon ends into the bead. When the glue sets, the ribbon will stay in place.

Variation
Dip-Dyed Chiffon Ribbon Threaded with Large Beads

If you want to use larger beads, they must be light in weight as heavier glass ones will drag on the ribbon when worn. The pretty faceted vintage plastic beads used here are ideal. A wider ribbon has been used, as the central hole in the bead is proportionately larger. This is one of the simplest projects in this book—try using a variety of ribbons, such as chiffon, satin, velvet, or taffeta, and choose beads from your collection to match.

Ribbon Rosebud Corsage

MATERIALS

2 x 20in (50cm) lengths of deep red-toned taffeta wired ribbon, 1½in (4cm) wide

1 yard (1m) burnt orange satin-edged ribbon, ¾in (2cm) wide

Soft jeweler's wire

2 gilded glass buttons with sewing holes on the back

Needle

Strong thread to match the ribbon tones

1 yard (1m) plum satin-edged ribbon, ¾in (2cm) wide

Brooch pin

Scissors

These ribbon roses in gentle tones, framed with a rosette of satin-edged ribbon, make the perfect corsage. The ribbon used for the roses has a fine, soft wire running down each edge. Pulling one of these wires gathers the edge, while the ungathered wired edge can be arranged into ruffles and folds. Make a bold statement and wear two together or attach them to a plain silk evening bag. They would look great used to hold a silk scarf or pashmina in place, or would work well as a hair adornment, especially if the ribbon color matches your outfit.

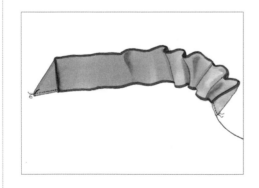

1 Take one length of taffeta wired ribbon and turn the ends of the ribbon over, sewing them neatly in place with a needle and thread. Pull the wire slightly at one end and bend it over to secure it, then pull the wire at the other end tightly, making sure you don't lose the wire protruding at the beginning.

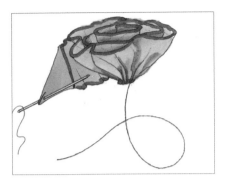

2 When the ribbon has been pulled tightly, turn it around on itself into a "rose." Sew the base together tightly as you turn and twist the protruding wires together to secure. Repeat steps 1–2 to make the second rose.

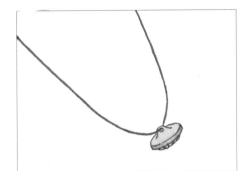

3 Cut a 6in (15cm) length of wire and thread halfway through the back of the glass button.

4 Fold the wire in half and twist tightly together so that the button is held securely and you have a long twisted tail.

5 Make a hole in the base of one of the roses with the eye end of the needle and push the wire tail on the button through this hole. Pull tightly so that the button sits snugly in the inside base of the rose. Repeat for the second rose.

6 Turn the rose upside down, twist the wire around, and hold against the base where the wire emerges. Start to loop the plum satin-edged ribbon around the base of the flower, sewing each loop and twist of the wire in place as you go.

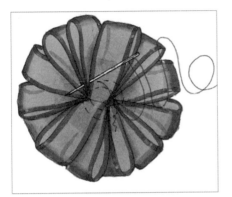

7 When all the ribbon has been looped evenly around the base of the rose, finish with a few holding stitches. The wire holding the button will be completely hidden by the ribbon folds.

8 Place the brooch pin centrally onto the back of the rosette and sew in place. Stitch first through the holes in the pin, then oversew the metal bar to make it secure. Finish off neatly and cut off the excess thread. Repeat steps 6–8 to make the second corsage with the burnt orange satin-edge ribbon.

Stuffed Fabric Bead Bracelet

MATERIALS

Circular paper template, 2½in (6cm) in diameter

Scraps of shiny fabric, in gold, pink, and silver

Pins

Needle

Strong thread, in colors to match the fabric

Cotton or polyester batting (wadding)

Pencil

Beading elastic

Needle with large eye

9 glass pearls, 1/16in (2mm) in diameter

1 crimp tube, 1/8in (3mm)

Scissors

Flat-nosed pliers

A perfect patchwork project! This method of creating beads originated in the Indian subcontinent and is a highly decorative technique requiring only the simplest of sewing skills. You can make any style of bead depending on the fabric you have—you can use plain or patterned cotton, exotic silks, or luxurious satins. If you are hesitating about taking a much-loved but rather worn dress to the thrift store, think again. Why not turn it into a special necklace? You could even intersperse the beads you have made with buttons from another favorite garment.

Crafter's tip In step 4, you will probably have to unthread the needle each time you thread a pearl in place as the central hole will not be large enough to take both needle and elastic.

1 Lay the paper template on the fabric and pin in place. Cut out three gold, three pink, and three silver circles. Turn over a small hem and sew a running stitch all around the edge.

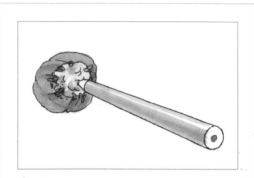

2 Pull the thread gently to make the circle into a little pouch, leaving the central hole slightly open. Stuff the pouch with enough batting (wadding) to make a round bead (it helps to use a pencil to push the batting in place).

3 When the bead is stuffed tightly, pull the thread to close the opening. Oversew for a few stitches, bringing the edges together to secure, and cut off the thread. Make up all the beads in this manner.

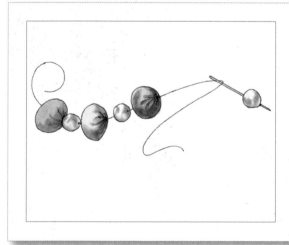

4 Cut a 20in (50cm) length of beading elastic and thread through the needle with the large eye. You may have to flatten the end of the elastic between your fingers to make it fit through the eye of the needle. Push the needle through the center of the stuffed beads and thread them alternately with the glass pearls. When all beads and pearls are in place, thread the elastic ends through opposite ends of the crimp tube, pull to tighten the bracelet, and press the crimp with the flat-nosed pliers. Cut off the excess elastic.

Variation
Fabric Bead Necklace

If you want to make an everyday necklace using the same technique, use patterned pieces of cotton. It takes some time to sew the beads, so if you want to make a longer necklace, add some matching wooden beads which are a similar size to the fabric version. The pale blue ones used here started off as natural wood color but have been immersed in a cold-water dye bath for 30 minutes to reach the desired tone. As with the bracelet, they can be threaded onto beading elastic, which gives them the advantage of being able to stretch around the neck. For a longer piece of jewelry, it is probably best to thread the beads on a waxed linen thread and tie a secure knot to close.

Moonstone
Bracelet

MATERIALS

1 yard (1m) eau-de-nil silk ribbon,
⅜in (8mm) wide

Needle (with an eye large enough to thread the ribbon but small enough to fit through the bead hole)

27 moonstone beads, ¼in (5mm) in diameter

1 pale blue button

Scissors

White craft glue

Moonstone is a beautiful semi-precious stone. It appears to exude an almost magical silvery light—hence its name. To enhance this quality, it is important not to overwhelm the stone with strong color or complicated design. Here, the simple beads have been threaded and knotted onto a pale eau-de-nil narrow silk ribbon. Make sure that your beads have a central hole large enough for the needle and ribbon to pass through. You will need to adjust the length of your bracelet to fit. A small button is used to finish the bracelet before the ribbon ends are tied into a decorative bow.

Crafter's tip When knotting, you will need at least twice as much ribbon as the length of your necklace.

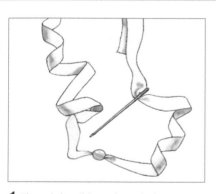

1 Thread the ribbon though the needle and pass a bead centrally onto the ribbon.

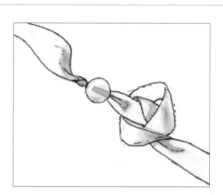

2 Tie a single knot in the ribbon on each side of the bead and close to it.

3 Continue threading the beads onto the ribbon either side of the central bead with tight knots against each bead until you have 25 in place. Make a final knot after each last bead at both ends.

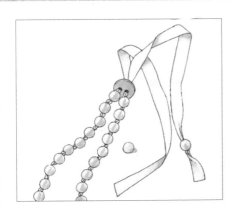

4 Pass the two ribbon ends through the two holes in the button from behind. Thread one more bead on each ribbon end and make a final knot after these beads. Cut off the excess ribbon, leaving a ½in (1cm) tail. Add a smear of white glue along this edge to seal the edges, then, when dry, cut again to make a neat and unfrayed end. To fasten the bracelet, tie the ribbon ends into a secure bow.

Suppliers

Sewing and craft supplies

United States

A.C. Moore
www.acmoore.com

Art Supplies Online
www.artsuppliesonline.com

Crafts, Etc.
www.craftsetc.com

Hobby Lobby
www.hobbylobby.com

Jo-Ann Fabric and Craft Stores
www.joann.com

Michaels
www.michaels.com

Purl Soho
www.purlsoho.com

United Kingdom

Blooming Felt
www.bloomingfelt.co.uk

The Cloth House
www.clothhouse.com

Coats Crafts
www.coatscrafts.co.uk

HobbyCraft
www.hobbycraft.co.uk

John Lewis
www.johnlewis.com

Kleins
www.kleins.co.uk

MacCulloch & Wallis
www.macculloch-wallis.co.uk

The Sewing Box
www.sewing-box.co.uk

VV Rouleaux
www.vvrouleaux.com

Beads and jeweler's tools

United States

Atlanta Bead Company
www.atlantabeadcompany.com

Beadaholique
www.beadaholique.com

Beadalon
www.beadalon.com

The Beadin' Path
www.beadinpath.com

Beaducation
www.beaducation.com

Beadworks
www.beadworks.com

Fire Mountain Gems and Beads
www.firemountaingems.com

Great Craft Works
www.greatcraftworks.com

Marvin Schwab, The Bead
Warehouse
www.thebeadwarehouse.com

National Jewelers Supplies
www.nationaljewelerssupplies.com

Phoenix Beads, Jewelry and Parts
www.phoenixbeads.com

Rings and Things
www.rings-things.com

Rio Grande
www.riogrande.com

Whimbeads
www.whimbeads.com

United Kingdom

Bead Addict
www.beadaddict.co.uk

Bead Aura
www.beadaura.co.uk

Beads Direct
www.beadsdirect.co.uk

The Bead Shop
www.beadshopscotland.co.uk

Beadworks Bead Shop
www.beadworks.co.uk

Bellore
www.bellore.co.uk

Bijoux Beads
www.bijouxbeads.co.uk

Crystals
www.crystalshop.co.uk

E-Beads
www.e-beads.co.uk

Jencel
www.jencel.co.uk

London Bead Company
www.londonbeadco.co.uk

London Bead Shop
www.londonbeadshop.co.uk

Spangles
www.spangles4beads.co.uk

Index

Acknowledgments

I would like to thank my husband Heini Schneebeli and my good
friend Gloria Nicol for taking the brilliant photographs in this book.
I really appreciate the lovely step-by-step drawings by Kate
Simunek. A big thank you to my publisher Cindy Richards for
taking on my ideas and commissioning this book, and lastly as ever,
so many thanks to my editor Gillian Haslam for her soothing
influence, calm advice, and seamless editing.